HAL•LEONARD®
GUITAR
PLAY-ALONG

AUDIO
ACCESS
INCLUDED

VOL. 11

PLAYBACK+
Speed • Pitch • Balance • Loop

To access audio visit:
www.halleonard.com/mylibrary

Enter Code
8055-5443-5595-4047

Tracking, mixing, and mastering by
Jake Johnson
All guitars by Doug Boduch
Bass by Tom McGirr
Keyboards by Warren Wiegratz
Drums by Scott Schroedl

ISBN: 978-0-634-05631-4

Visit Hal Leonard Online at
www.halleonard.com

Contact Us:
Hal Leonard
7777 West Bluemound Road
Milwaukee, WI 53213
Email: info@halleonard.com

In Europe contact:
Hal Leonard Europe Limited
Distribution Centre, Newmarket Road
Bury St Edmunds, Suffolk, IP33 3YB
Email: info@halleonardeurope.com

In Australia contact:
Hal Leonard Australia Pty. Ltd.
4 Lentara Court
Cheltenham, Victoria, 3192 Australia
Email: info@halleonard.com.au

GUITAR PLAY-ALONG

AUDIO ACCESS INCLUDED

VOL. 11

Early ROCK

CONTENTS

Guitar Notation Legend

Notes:

THE MUSICAL STAFF shows pitches and rhythms and is divided by bar lines into measures. Pitches are named after the first seven letters of the alphabet.

TABLATURE graphically represents the guitar fingerboard. Each horizontal line represents a string, and each number represents a fret.

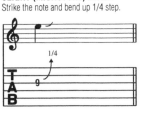
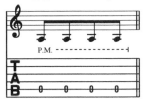

4th string, 2nd fret   1st & 2nd strings open, played together   open D chord

HALF-STEP BEND: Strike the note and bend up 1/2 step.

WHOLE-STEP BEND: Strike the note and bend up one step.

GRACE NOTE BEND: Strike the note and bend up as indicated. The first note does not take up any time.

SLIGHT (MICROTONE) BEND: Strike the note and bend up 1/4 step.

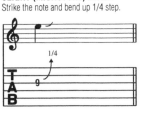

BEND AND RELEASE: Strike the note and bend up as indicated, then release back to the original note. Only the first note is struck.

PRE-BEND: Bend the note as indicated, then strike it.

VIBRATO: The string is vibrated by rapidly bending and releasing the note with the fretting hand.

PALM MUTING: The note is partially muted by the pick hand lightly touching the string(s) just before the bridge.

HAMMER-ON: Strike the first (lower) note with one finger, then sound the higher note (on the same string) with another finger by fretting it without picking.

PULL-OFF: Place both fingers on the notes to be sounded. Strike the first note and without picking, pull the finger off to sound the second (lower) note.

LEGATO SLIDE: Strike the first note and then slide the same fret-hand finger up or down to the second note. The second note is not struck.

SHIFT SLIDE: Same as legato slide, except the second note is struck.

PINCH HARMONIC: The note is fretted normally and a harmonic is produced by adding the edge of the thumb or the tip of the index finger of the pick hand to the normal pick attack.

TRILL: Very rapidly alternate between the notes indicated by continuously hammering on and pulling off.

TAPPING: Hammer ("tap") the fret indicated with the pick-hand index or middle finger and pull off to the note fretted by the fret hand.

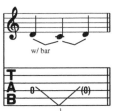

NATURAL HARMONIC: Strike the note while the fret-hand lightly touches the string directly over the fret indicated.

TREMOLO PICKING: The note is picked as rapidly and continuously as possible.

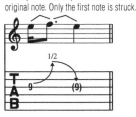

VIBRATO BAR DIVE AND RETURN: The pitch of the note or chord is dropped a specified number of steps (in rhythm) then returned to the original pitch.

VIBRATO BAR SCOOP: Depress the bar just before striking the note, then quickly release the bar.

VIBRATO BAR DIP: Strike the note and then immediately drop a specified number of steps, then release back to the original pitch.

Additional Musical Definitions

 (accent) • Accentuate note (play it louder)

 *(staccato)* • Play the note short

D.S. al Coda • Go back to the sign (𝄋), then play until the measure marked *"To Coda,"* then skip to the section labelled *"Coda."*

D.C. al Fine • Go back to the beginning of the song and play until the measure marked *"Fine"* (end).

Fill • Label used to identify a brief melodic figure which is to be inserted into the arrangement.

N.C. • Instrument is silent (drops out).

 • Repeat measures between signs.

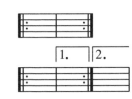 • When a repeated section has different endings, play the first ending only the first time and the second ending only the second time.

Fun, Fun, Fun

Words and Music by Brian Wilson and Mike Love

Tune down 1/2 step:
(low to high) E♭-A♭-D♭-G♭-B♭-E♭

Intro
Moderately fast ♩ = 168

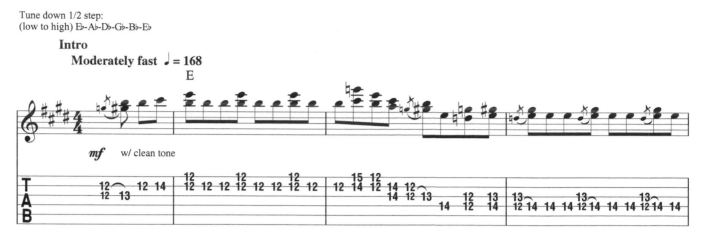

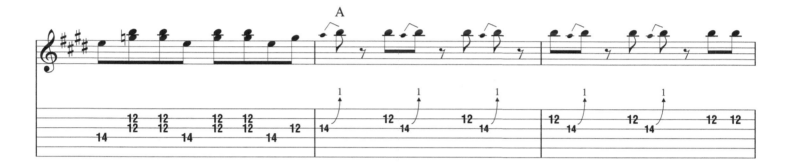

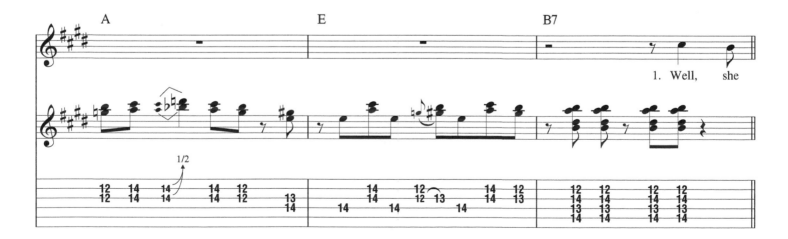

1. Well, she

Verse

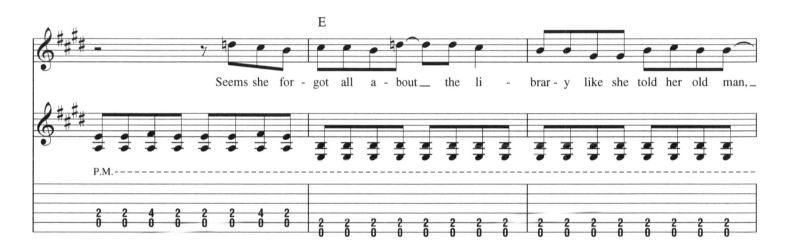

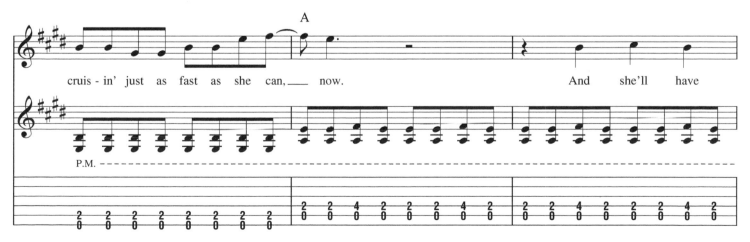

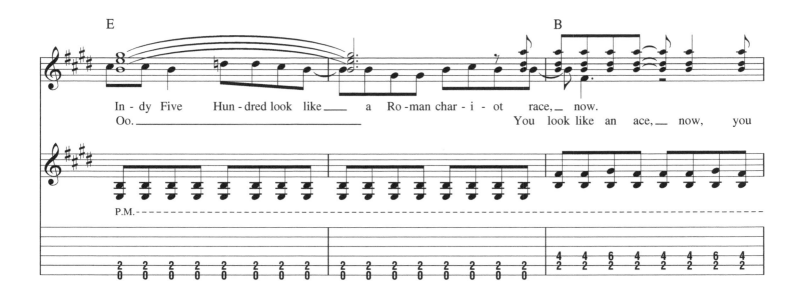

In - dy Five Hun - dred look like ___ a Ro - man char - i - ot race, ___ now.
Oo. _____ You look like an ace, ___ now, you

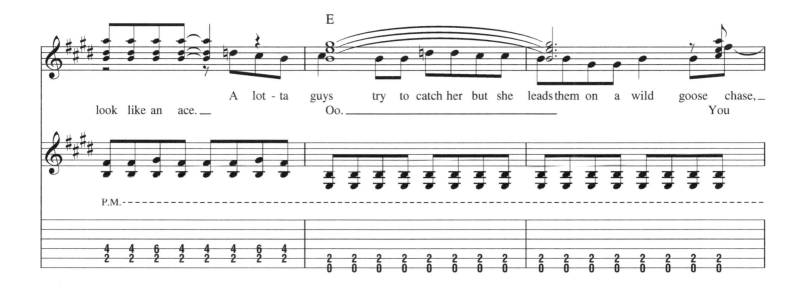

A lot - ta guys try to catch her but she leads them on a wild goose chase, ___
look like an ace. ___ Oo. _____ You

___ now. And she'll have fun, fun, fun till her
drive like an ace, ___ now, you drive like an ace. ___ Fun, fun, fun till her
(Fun, fun, fun till her

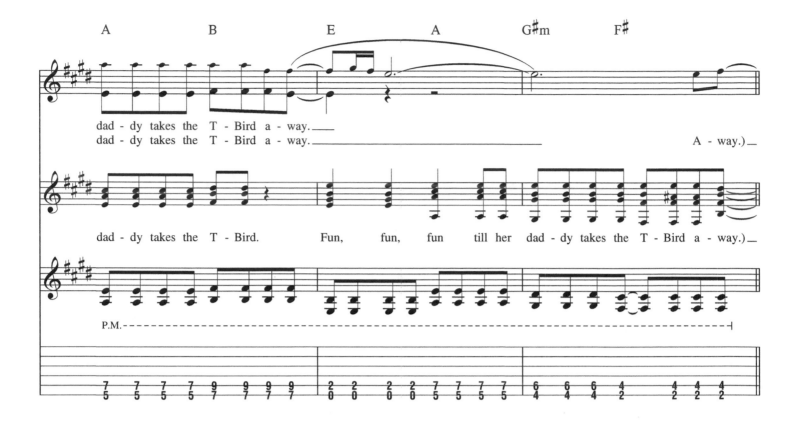

dad - dy takes the T - Bird a - way.___
dad - dy takes the T - Bird a - way._____
A - way.) __

dad - dy takes the T - Bird.   Fun,   fun,   fun   till her   dad - dy takes the T - Bird a - way.) __

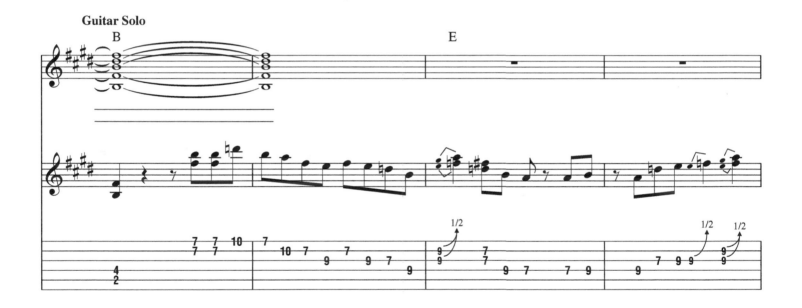

Guitar Solo

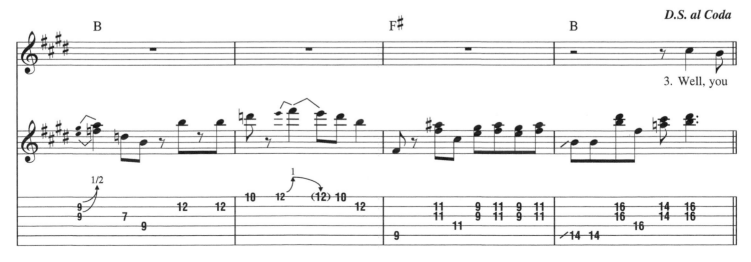

D.S. al Coda

3. Well, you

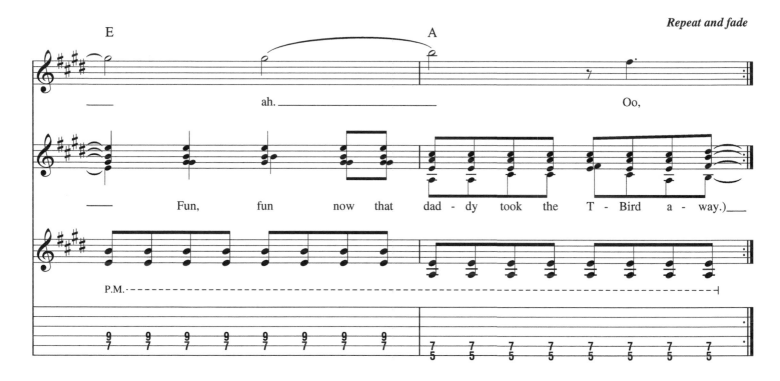

Additional Lyrics

3. Well, you knew all along
   That your dad was gettin' wise to you, now.
   (You shouldn't have lied, now, you shouldn't have lied.)
   And since he took your set of keys
   You've been thinkin' that your fun is all through, now.
   (You shouldn't have lied, now, you shouldn't have lied.)
   But you can come along with me
   'Cause we got a lotta things to do now.
   (You shouldn't have lied, now, you shouldn't have lied.)
   And we'll..

Hound Dog

Words and Music by Jerry Leiber and Mike Stoller

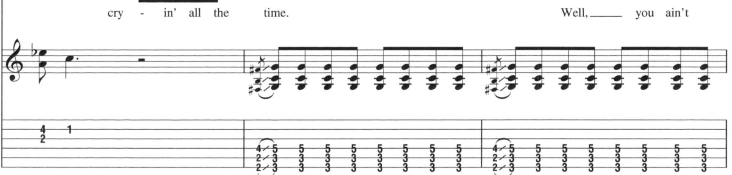

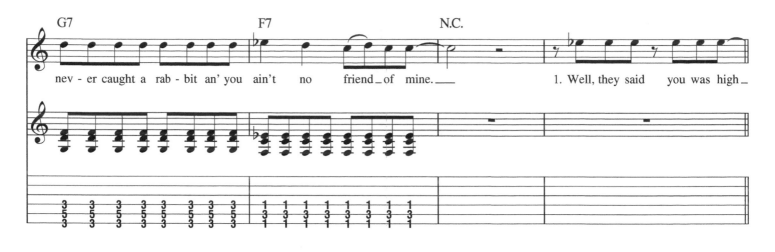

nev - er caught a rab - bit an' you ain't no friend _ of mine. ____ 1. Well, they said you was high _

Verse

____ classed. ____ Well, that _ was just a lie. Yeah, they said you was high _

____ class. ____ Well, that _ was just a lie. Yeah, __ you ain't

To Coda 1

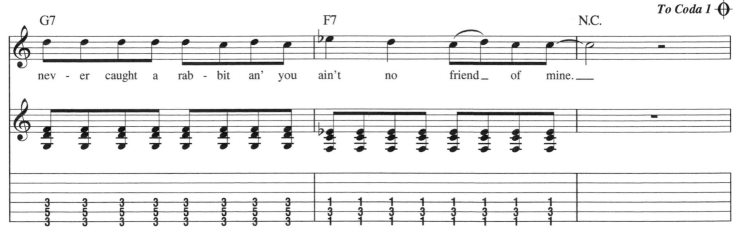

nev - er caught a rab - bit an' you ain't no friend _ of mine. ____

Chorus

You ain't noth - in' but a hound dog__ ah, cry - in' all the time.

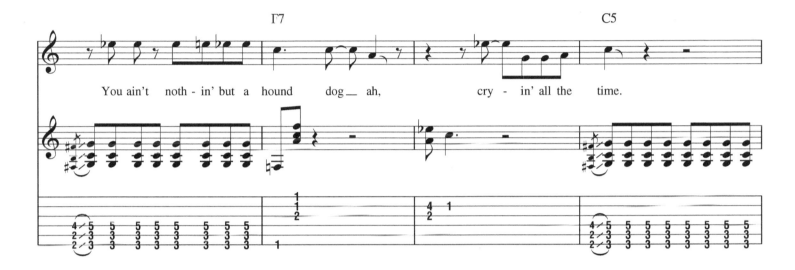

You ain't noth - in' but a hound dog__ ah, cry - in' all the time.

To Coda 2 ⊕

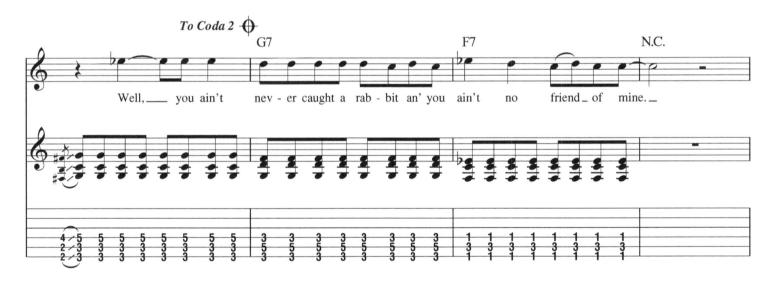

Well,__ you ain't nev - er caught a rab - bit an' you ain't no friend__ of mine.__

Guitar Solo

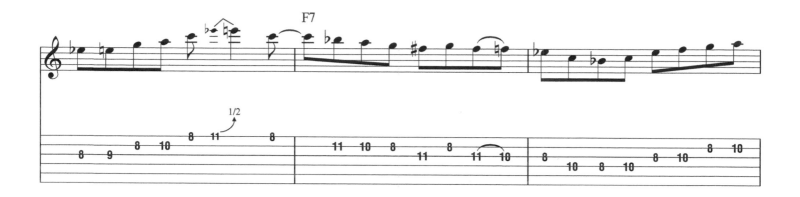

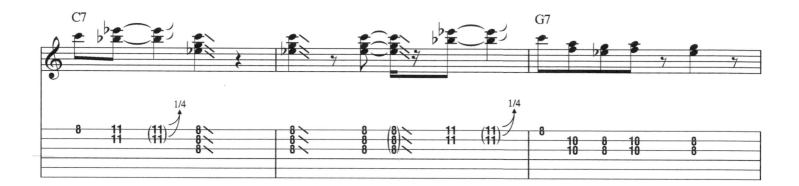

D.S. al Coda 1

2. Well, they said   you was   high___

Coda 1

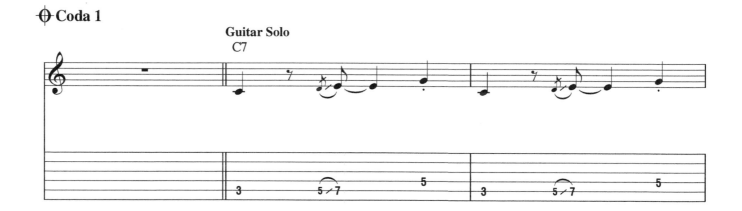

D.S. al Coda 2

3. Well, they said___ you was high___

Coda 2

nev-er caught a rab-bit; you ain't no friend___ of mine.___ *Spoken:* You ain't noth-in' but a hound dog.

Louie, Louie

Words and Music by Richard Berry

Intro

Moderate Rock ♩ = 124

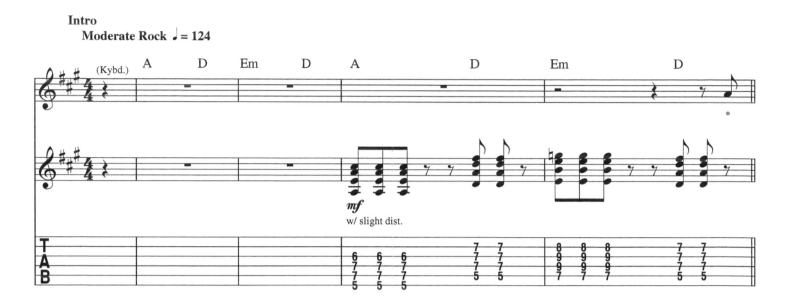

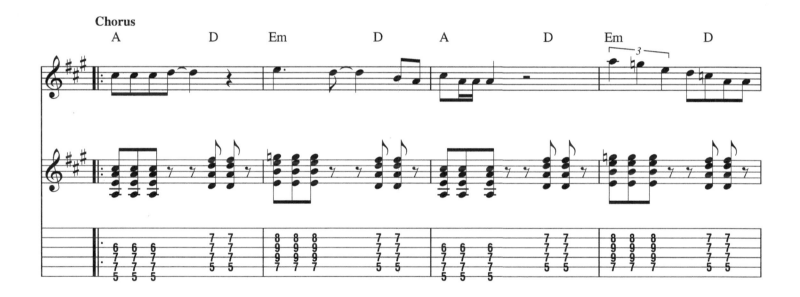

*Lyrics omitted at the request of the publisher.

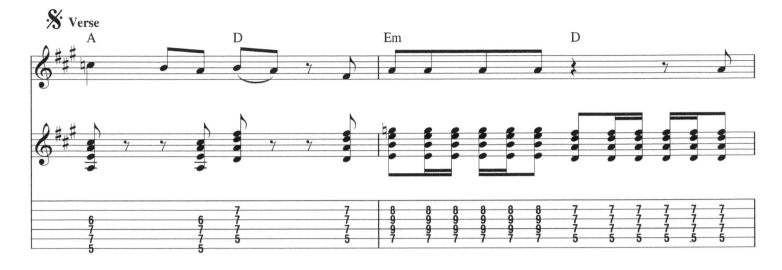

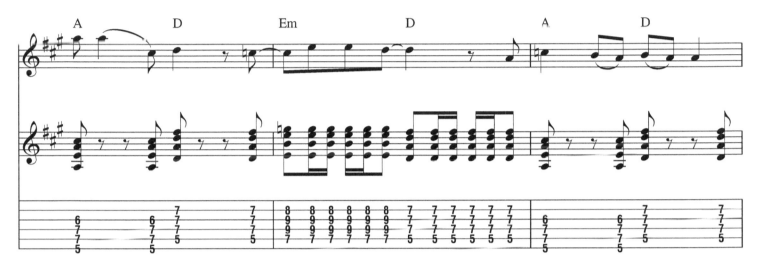

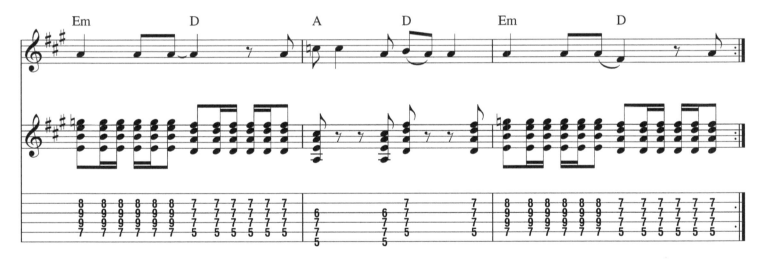

Chorus

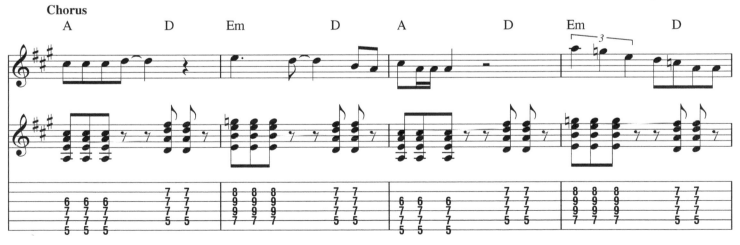

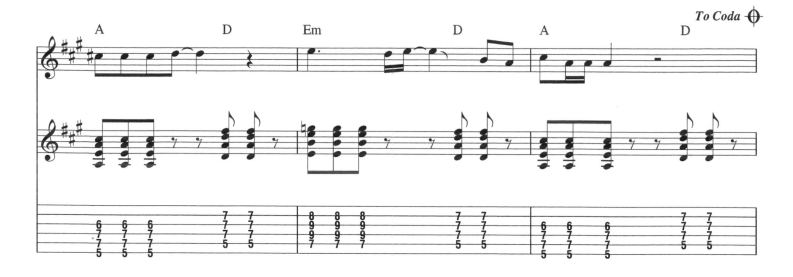

Guitar Solo

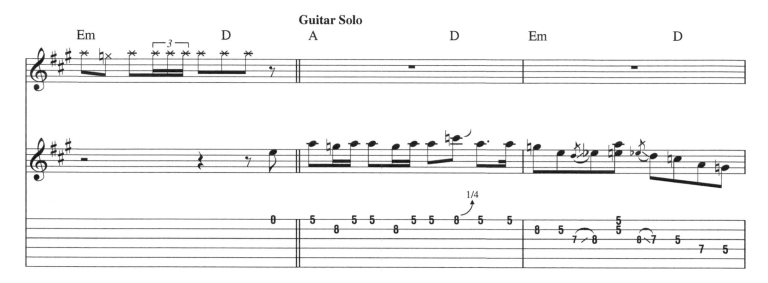

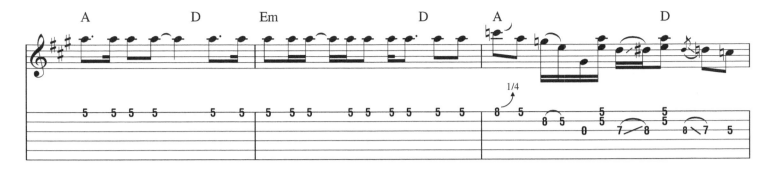

D.S. al Coda
(no repeat)

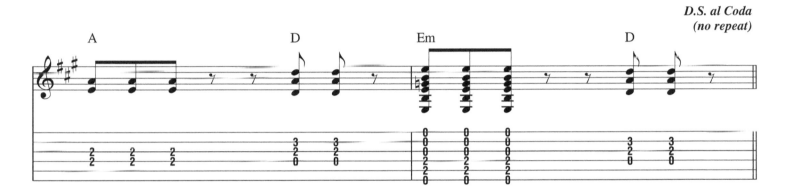

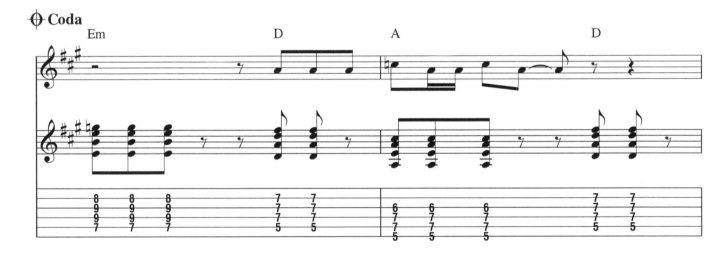

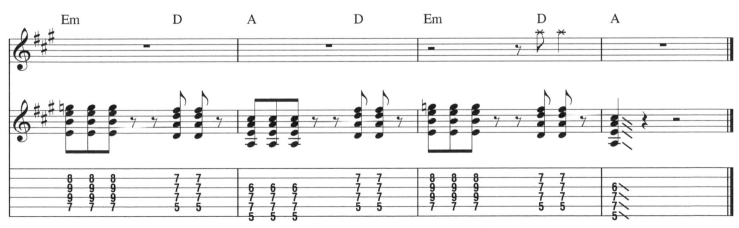

No Particular Place to Go

Words and Music by Chuck Berry

Cruis - in' and play - in' the ra - di - o

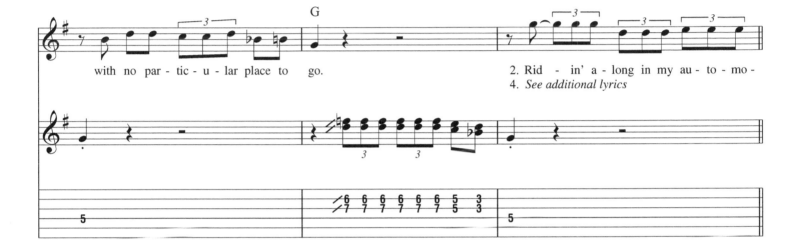

with no par - tic - u - lar place to go.

2. Rid - in' a - long in my au - to - mo -
4. *See additional lyrics*

Verse

bile, I's anx - ious to tell her the way I feel.

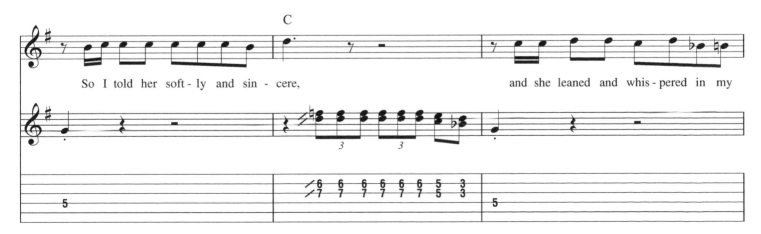

So I told her soft - ly and sin - cere, and she leaned and whis - pered in my

ear.   Cud - dl - in' more and driv - in' slow

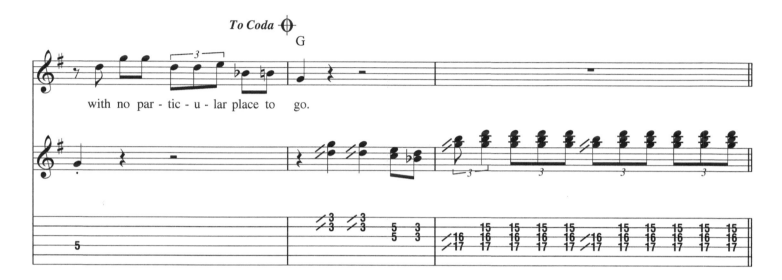

To Coda ⊕
G

with no par - tic - u - lar place to   go.

Guitar Solo
G

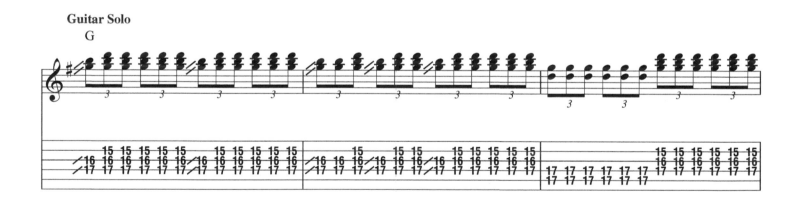

C

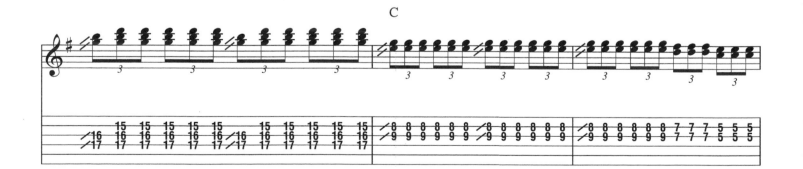

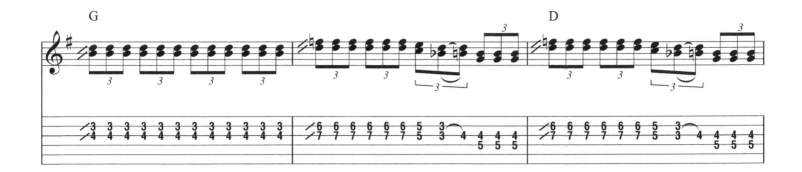

D.S. al Coda

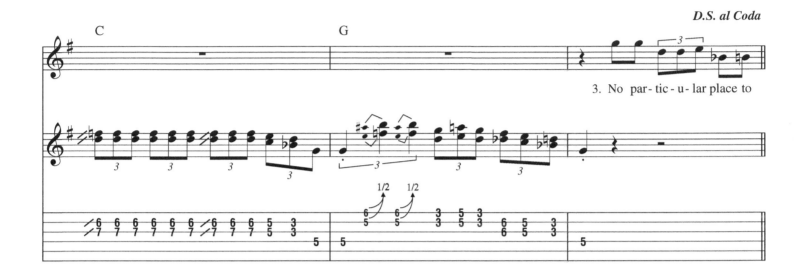

3. No par-tic-u-lar place to

Coda

Outro-Guitar Solo

go.

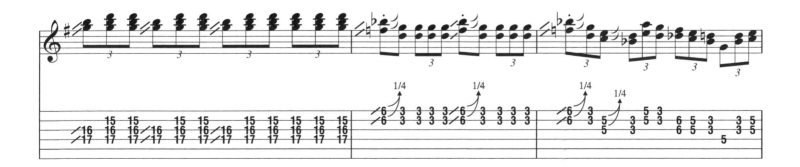

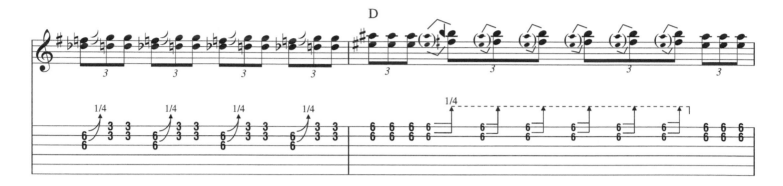

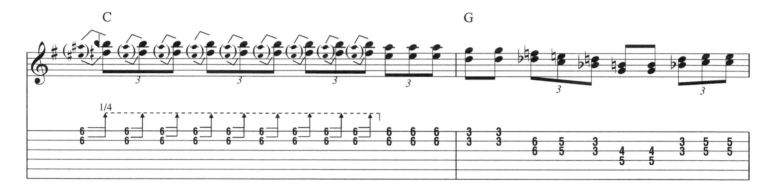

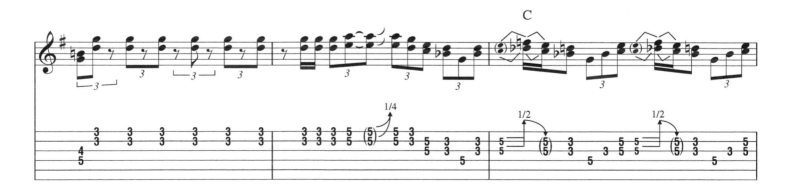

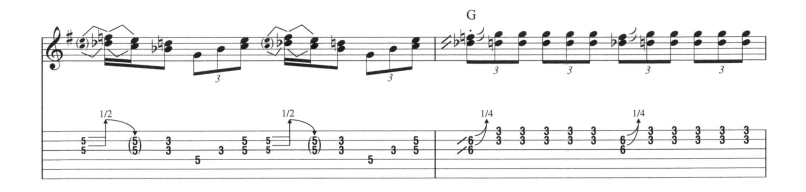

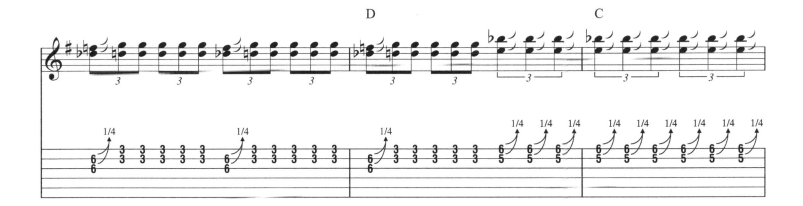

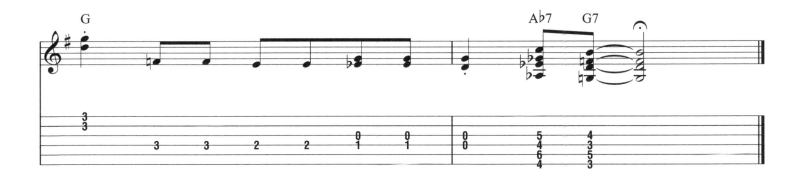

Additional Lyrics

3. No particular place to go,
   So we parked way out in the Kokomo.
   The night was young and the moon was gold,
   So we both decided to take a stroll.
   Can you imagine the way I felt?
   I couldn't unfasten her safety belt.

4. Ridin' along in my calaboose,
   Still tryin' to get her belt a loose.
   All the way home I held a grudge
   For the safety belt that wouldn't budge.
   Cruisin' and playin' the radio
   With no particular place to go.

Oh, Pretty Woman

Words and Music by Roy Orbison and Bill Dees

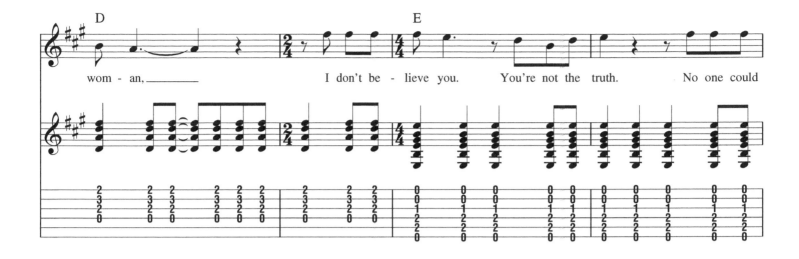

wom - an, _____   I don't be - lieve you.   You're not the truth.   No one could

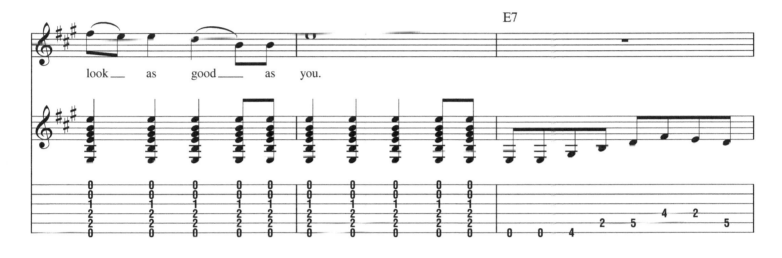

look __ as good __ as you.

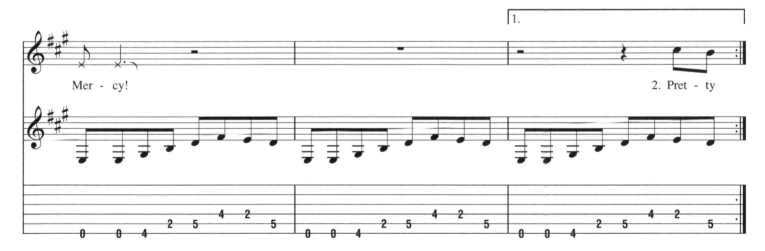

Mer - cy!   2. Pret - ty

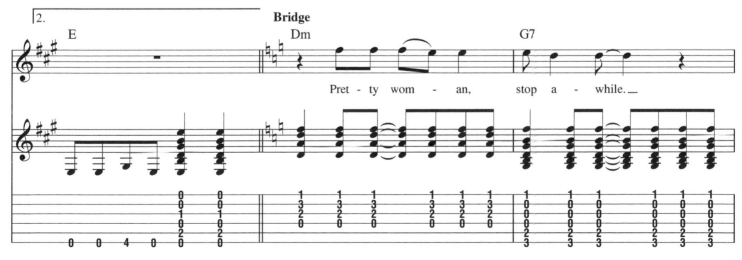

Pret - ty wom - an,   stop a - while. __

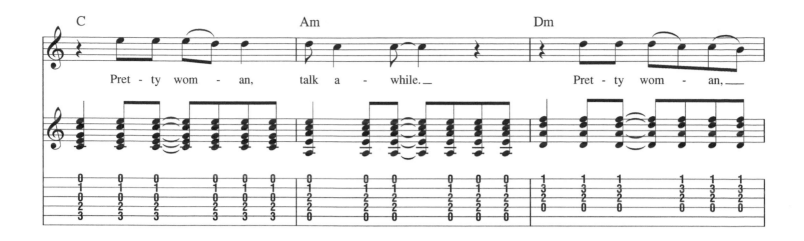

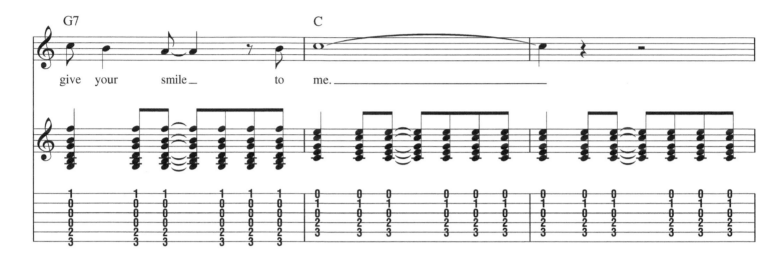

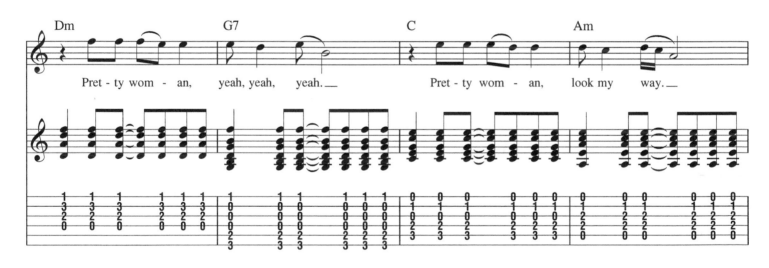

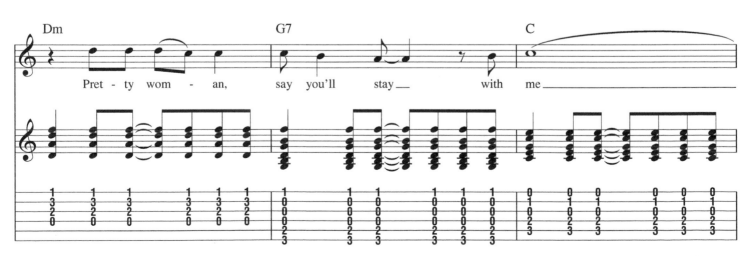

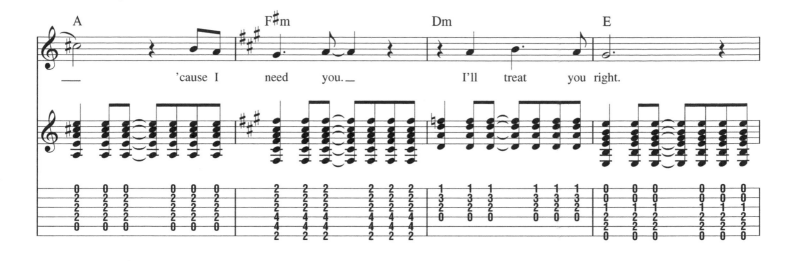

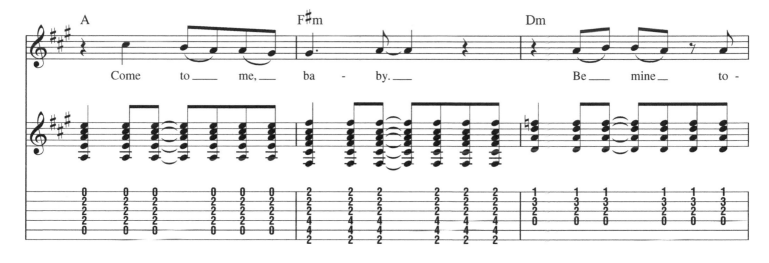

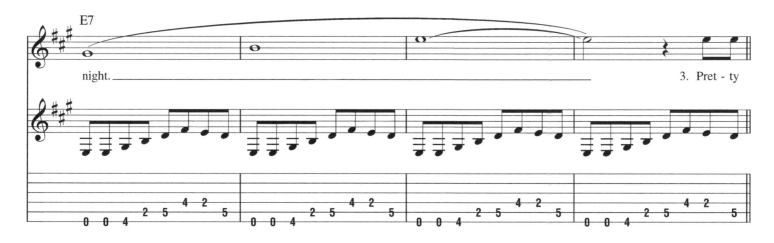

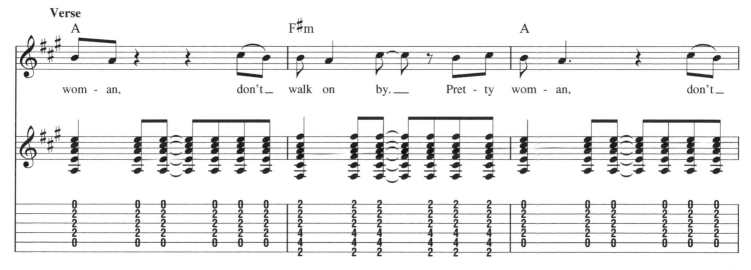

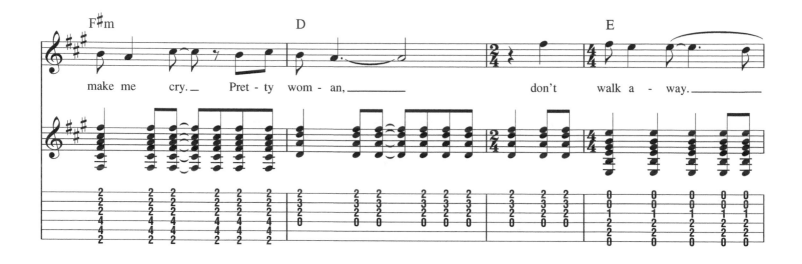

make me cry.__ Pret - ty wom - an,_____ don't walk a - way._____

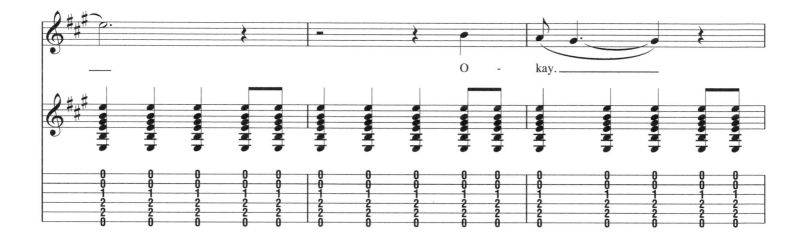

__ O - kay._____

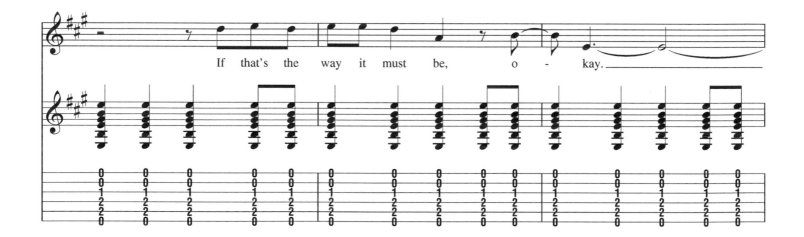

If that's the way it must be, o - kay._____

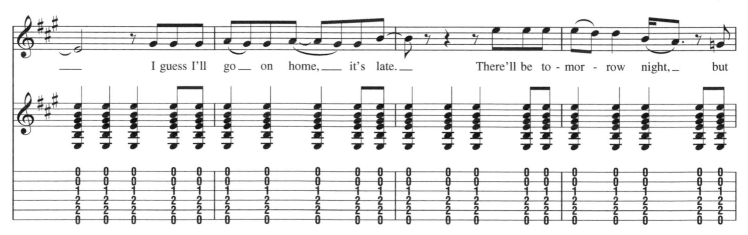

__ I guess I'll go__ on home,____ it's late.__ There'll be to - mor - row night,__ but

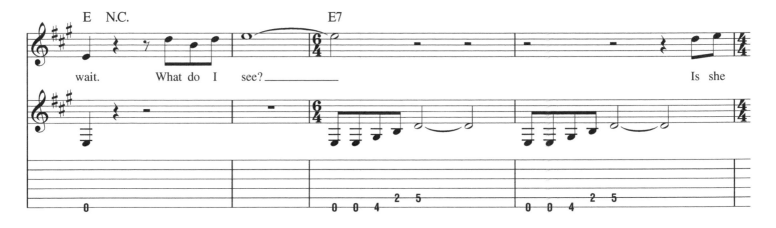

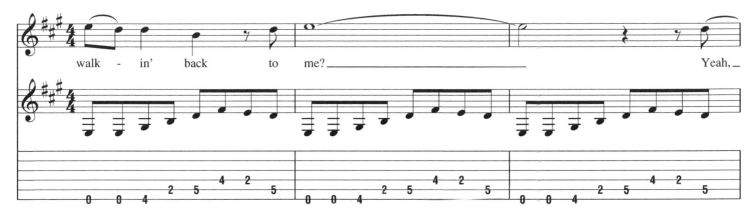

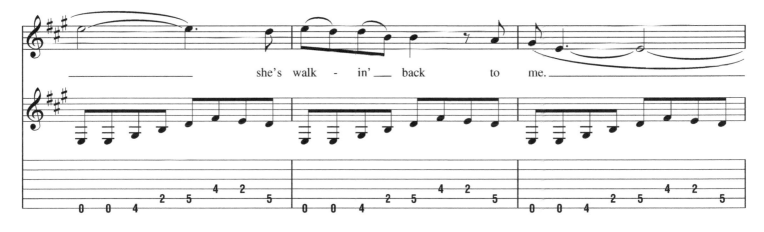

Additional Lyrics

2. Pretty woman, won't you pardon me?
   Pretty woman, I couldn't help but see;
   Pretty woman, that you look lovely as can be.
   Are you lonely just like me?

Rock Around the Clock

Words and Music by Max C. Freedman and Jimmy DeKnight

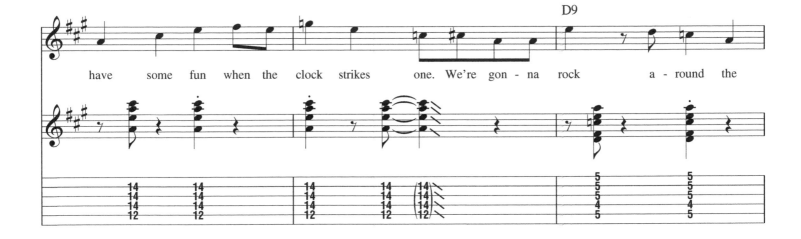

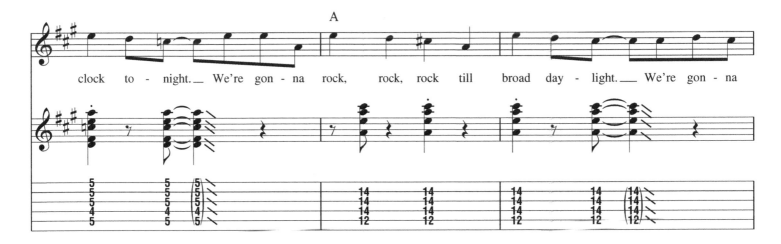

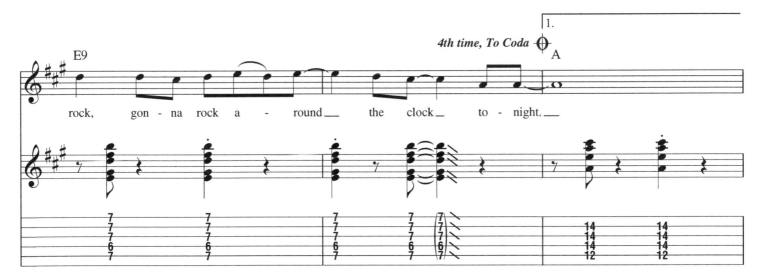

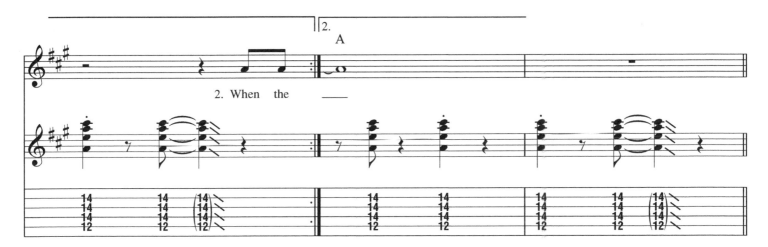

Guitar Solo

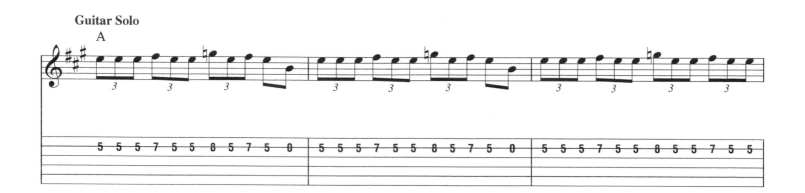

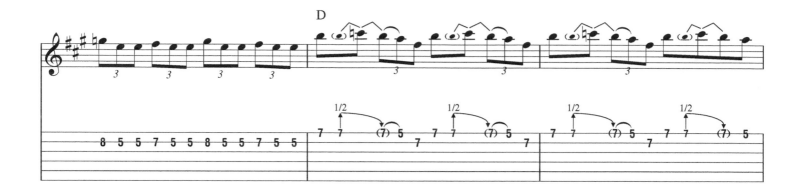

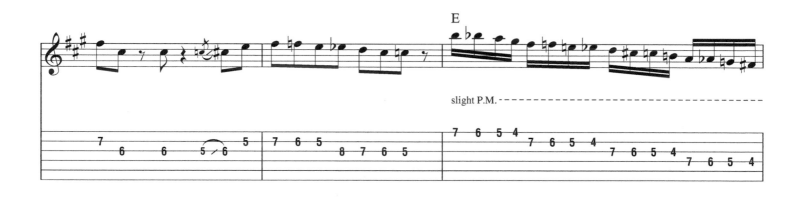

D.S. al Coda
(take repeat)

3. When the

⊕ Coda

Interlude

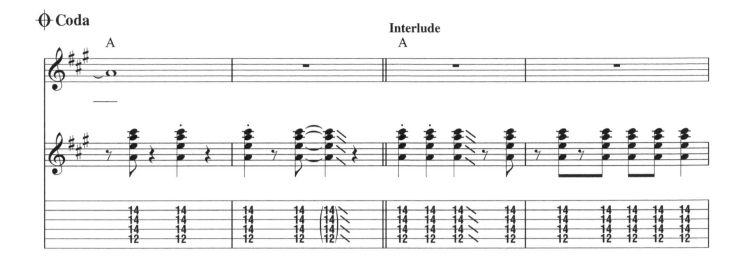

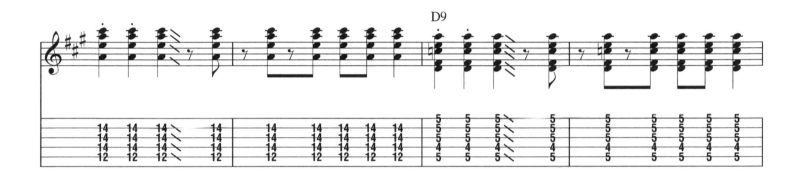

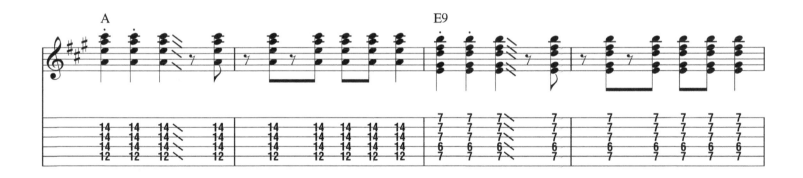

Verse

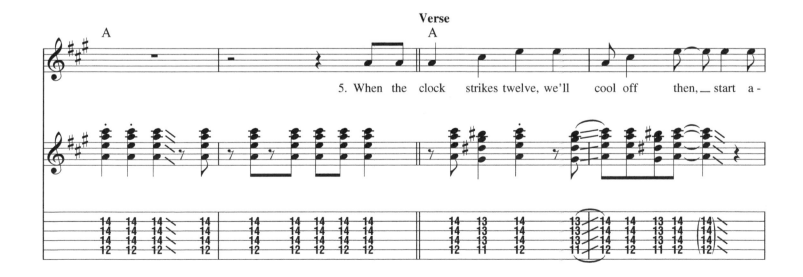

5. When the clock strikes twelve, we'll cool off then, ___ start a-

37

Additional Lyrics

2. When the clock strikes two, three and four,
   If the band slows down we'll yell for more.
   We're gonna rock around the clock tonight.
   We're gonna rock, rock, rock till broad daylight.
   We're gonna rock, gonna rock around the clock tonight.

3. When the chimes ring five, six and seven,
   We'll be right in seventh heaven.
   We're gonna rock around the clock tonight.
   We're gonna rock, rock, rock till broad daylight.
   We're gonna rock, gonna rock around the clock tonight.

4. When it's eight, nine, ten, eleven too,
   I'll be goin' strong and so will you.
   We're gonna rock around the clock tonight.
   We're gonna rock, rock, rock till broad daylight.
   We're gonna rock, gonna rock around the clock tonight.

Under the Boardwalk

Words and Music by Artie Resnick and Kenny Young

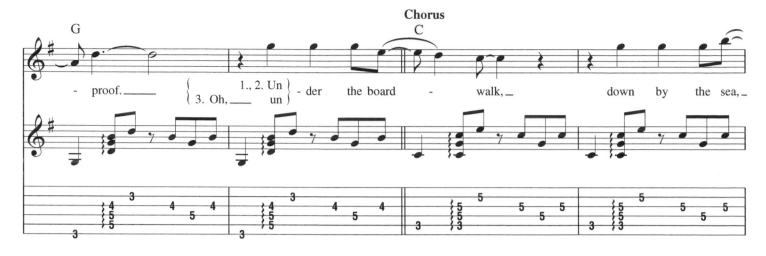

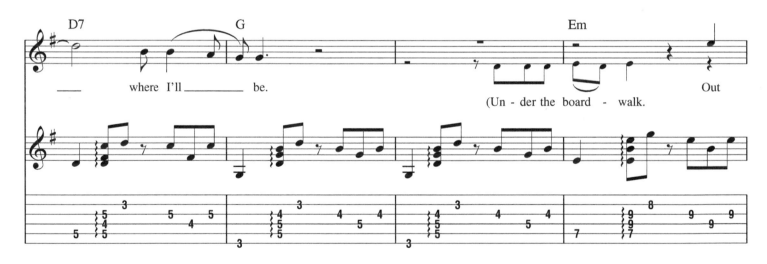

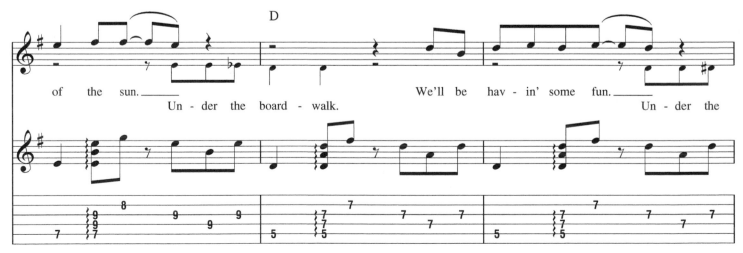

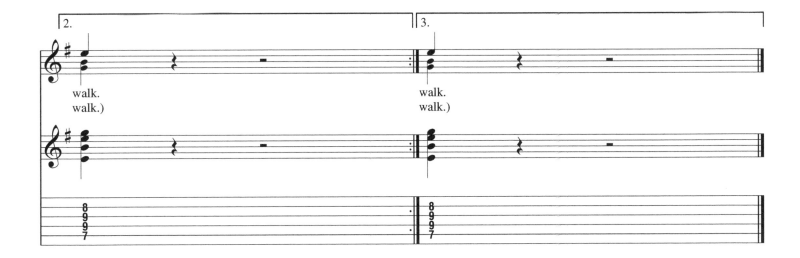

Additional Lyrics

2. From the park you hear the happy sound of the carousel,
   You can almost taste the hot dogs and french fries they sell.

Wild Thing

Words and Music by Chip Taylor

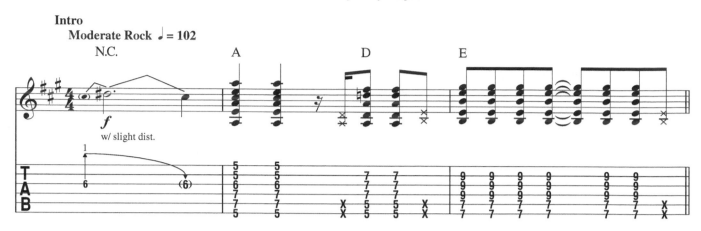

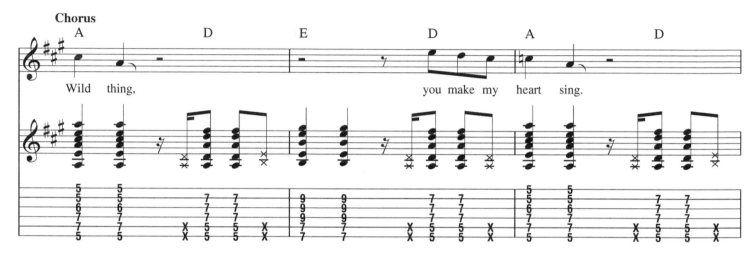

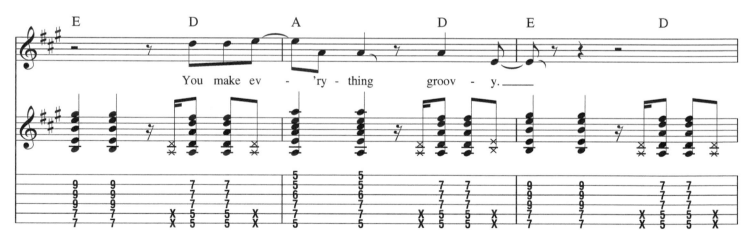

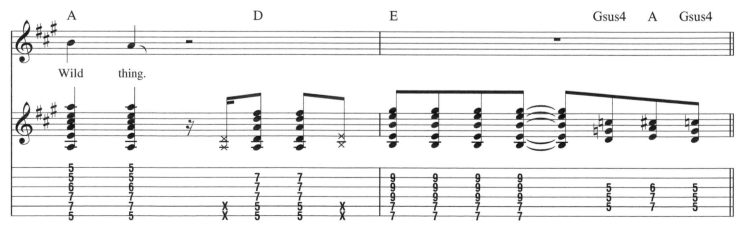

%. **Verse**

1. Wild thing,____ I think I love you,
2. Wild thing,____ I think you move me,

but I wan-na know____ for sure.

So, come on and

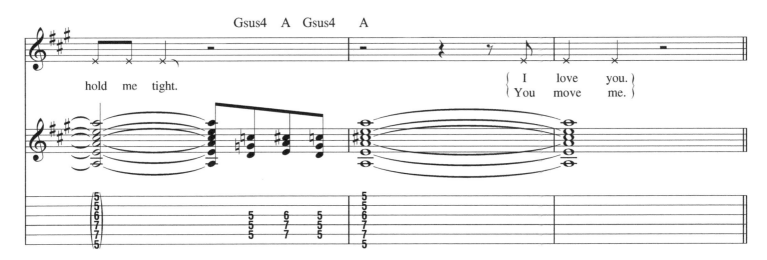

hold me tight.

{ I love you. }
{ You move me. }

Pre-Chorus

To Coda ⊕

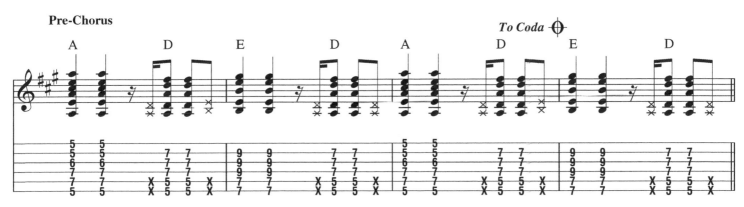

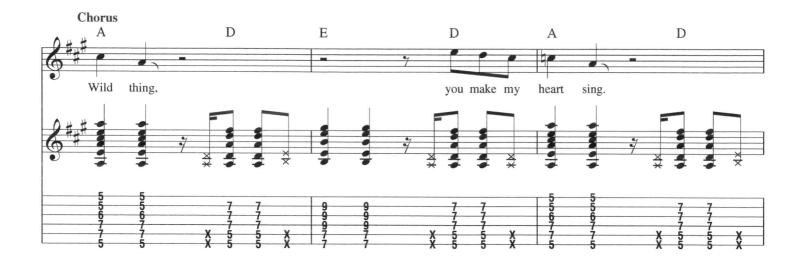

Wild thing,   you make my heart sing.

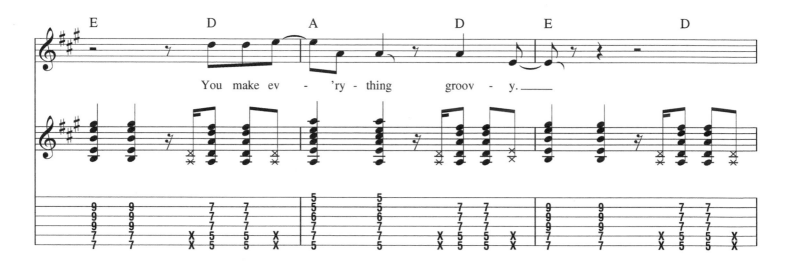

You make ev - 'ry - thing   groov - y. ____

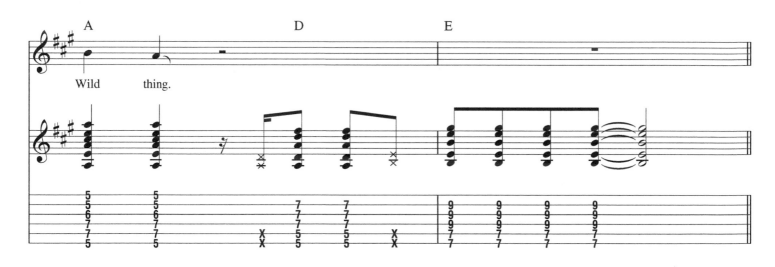

Wild   thing.

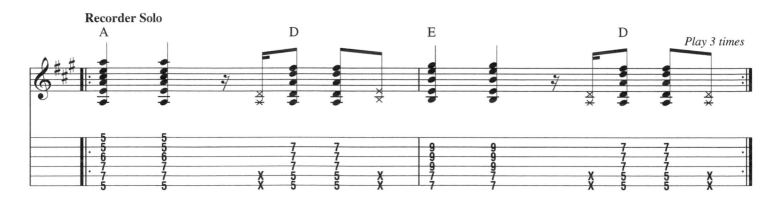

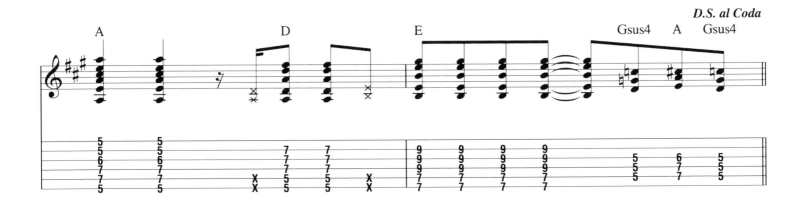

Coda

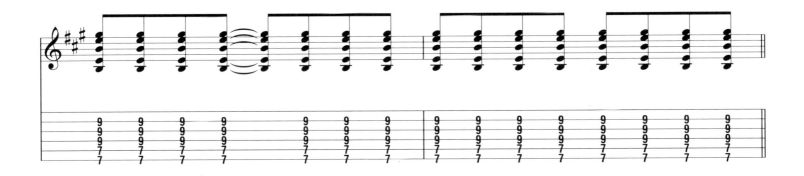

Outro-Chorus

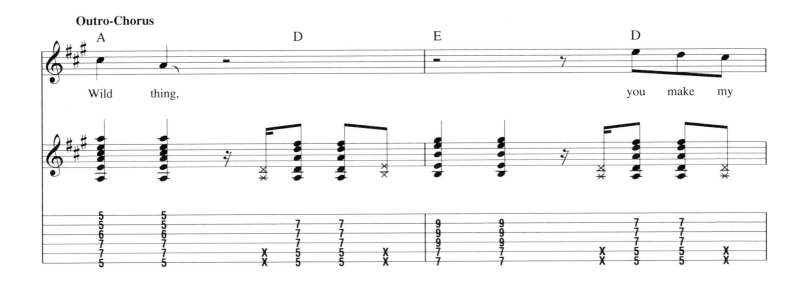

Wild thing, you make my

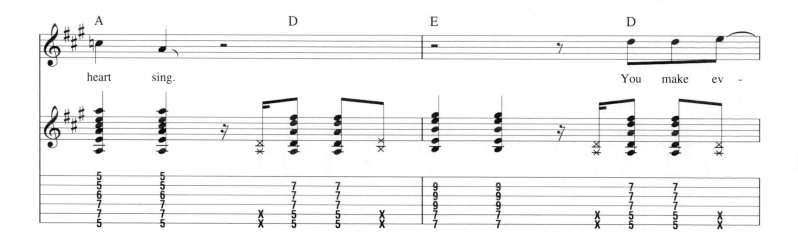

heart sing. You make ev -

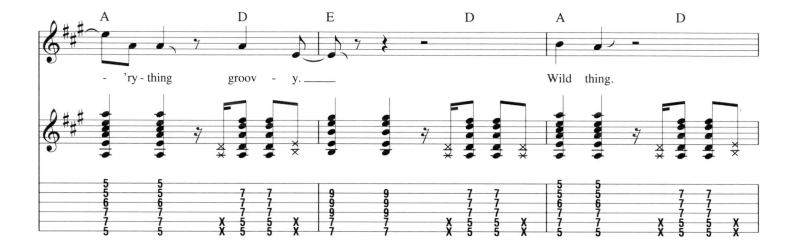

-'ry-thing groov - y. ___ Wild thing.

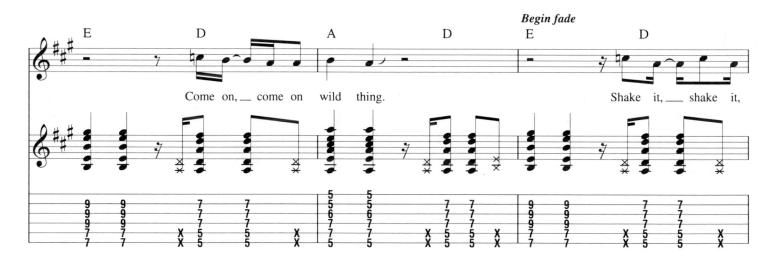

Begin fade

Come on, ___ come on wild thing. Shake it, ___ shake it,

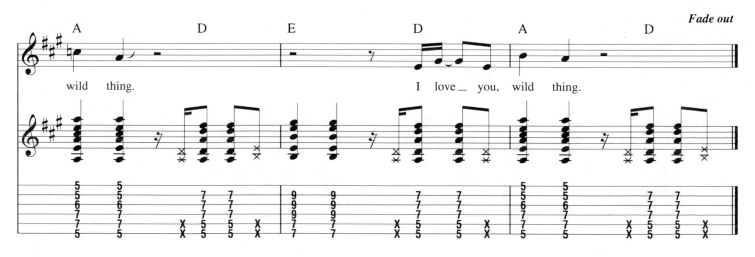

Fade out

wild thing. I love ___ you, wild thing.

HAL•LEONARD® GUITAR PLAY-ALONG

Complete song lists available online.

This series will help you play your favorite songs quickly and easily. Just follow the tab and listen to the audio to the hear how the guitar should sound, and then play along using the separate backing tracks. Audio files also include software to slow down the tempo without changing pitch. The melody and lyrics are included in the book so that you can sing or simply follow along.

INCLUDES TAB

VOL. 1 – ROCK	00699570 / $17.99
VOL. 2 – ACOUSTIC	00699569 / $16.99
VOL. 3 – HARD ROCK	00699573 / $17.99
VOL. 4 – POP/ROCK	00699571 / $16.99
VOL. 5 – THREE CHORD SONGS	00300985 / $16.99
VOL. 6 – '90S ROCK	00298615 / $16.99
VOL. 7 – BLUES	00699575 / $19.99
VOL. 8 – ROCK	00699585 / $16.99
VOL. 9 – EASY ACOUSTIC SONGS	00151708 / $16.99
VOL. 10 – ACOUSTIC	00699586 / $16.95
VOL. 11 – EARLY ROCK	00699579 / $15.99
VOL. 12 – ROCK POP	00291724 / $16.99
VOL. 14 – BLUES ROCK	00699582 / $16.99
VOL. 15 – R&B	00699583 / $17.99
VOL. 16 – JAZZ	00699584 / $16.99
VOL. 17 – COUNTRY	00699588 / $17.99
VOL. 18 – ACOUSTIC ROCK	00699577 / $15.95
VOL. 20 – ROCKABILLY	00699580 / $17.99
VOL. 21 – SANTANA	00174525 / $17.99
VOL. 22 – CHRISTMAS	00699600 / $15.99
VOL. 23 – SURF	00699635 / $17.99
VOL. 24 – ERIC CLAPTON	00699649 / $19.99
VOL. 25 – THE BEATLES	00198265 / $19.99
VOL. 26 – ELVIS PRESLEY	00699643 / $16.99
VOL. 27 – DAVID LEE ROTH	00699645 / $16.95
VOL. 28 – GREG KOCH	00699646 / $19.99
VOL. 29 – BOB SEGER	00699647 / $16.99
VOL. 30 – KISS	00699644 / $17.99
VOL. 32 – THE OFFSPRING	00699653 / $14.95
VOL. 33 – ACOUSTIC CLASSICS	00699656 / $19.99
VOL. 34 – CLASSIC ROCK	00699658 / $17.99
VOL. 35 – HAIR METAL	00699660 / $17.99
VOL. 36 – SOUTHERN ROCK	00699661 / $19.99
VOL. 37 – ACOUSTIC UNPLUGGED	00699662 / $22.99
VOL. 38 – BLUES	00699663 / $17.99
VOL. 39 – '80s METAL	00699664 / $17.99
VOL. 40 – INCUBUS	00699668 / $17.95
VOL. 41 – ERIC CLAPTON	00699669 / $17.99
VOL. 42 – COVER BAND HITS	00211597 / $16.99
VOL. 43 – LYNYRD SKYNYRD	00699681 / $22.99
VOL. 44 – JAZZ GREATS	00699689 / $16.99
VOL. 45 – TV THEMES	00699718 / $14.95
VOL. 46 – MAINSTREAM ROCK	00699722 / $16.95
VOL. 47 – JIMI HENDRIX SMASH HITS	00699723 / $19.99
VOL. 48 – AEROSMITH CLASSICS	00699724 / $17.99
VOL. 49 – STEVIE RAY VAUGHAN	00699725 / $17.99
VOL. 50 – VAN HALEN: 1978-1984	00110269 / $19.99
VOL. 51 – ALTERNATIVE '90s	00699727 / $14.99
VOL. 52 – FUNK	00699728 / $15.99
VOL. 53 – DISCO	00699729 / $14.99
VOL. 54 – HEAVY METAL	00699730 / $17.99
VOL. 55 – POP METAL	00699731 / $14.95
VOL. 57 – GUNS 'N' ROSES	00159922 / $19.99
VOL. 58 – BLINK 182	00699772 / $17.99
VOL. 59 – CHET ATKINS	00702347 / $17.99
VOL. 60 – 3 DOORS DOWN	00699774 / $14.95
VOL. 62 – CHRISTMAS CAROLS	00699798 / $12.95
VOL. 63 – CREEDENCE CLEARWATER REVIVAL	00699802 / $17.99
VOL. 64 – ULTIMATE OZZY OSBOURNE	00699803 / $19.99
VOL. 66 – THE ROLLING STONES	00699807 / $19.99
VOL. 67 – BLACK SABBATH	00699808 / $17.99
VOL. 68 – PINK FLOYD – DARK SIDE OF THE MOON	00699809 / $17.99
VOL. 71 – CHRISTIAN ROCK	00699824 / $14.95

VOL. 73 – BLUESY ROCK	00699829 / $17.99
VOL. 74 – SIMPLE STRUMMING SONGS	00151706 / $19.99
VOL. 75 – TOM PETTY	00699882 / $19.99
VOL. 76 – COUNTRY HITS	00699884 / $16.99
VOL. 77 – BLUEGRASS	00699910 / $17.99
VOL. 78 – NIRVANA	00700132 / $17.99
VOL. 79 – NEIL YOUNG	00700133 / $24.99
VOL. 81 – ROCK ANTHOLOGY	00700176 / $22.99
VOL. 82 – EASY ROCK SONGS	00700177 / $17.99
VOL. 84 – STEELY DAN	00700200 / $19.99
VOL. 85 – THE POLICE	00700269 / $16.99
VOL. 86 – BOSTON	00700465 / $19.99
VOL. 87 – ACOUSTIC WOMEN	00700763 / $14.99
VOL. 88 – GRUNGE	00700467 / $16.99
VOL. 89 – REGGAE	00700468 / $15.99
VOL. 90 – CLASSICAL POP	00700469 / $14.99
VOL. 91 – BLUES INSTRUMENTALS	00700505 / $19.99
VOL. 92 – EARLY ROCK INSTRUMENTALS	00700506 / $17.99
VOL. 93 – ROCK INSTRUMENTALS	00700507 / $17.99
VOL. 94 – SLOW BLUES	00700508 / $16.99
VOL. 95 – BLUES CLASSICS	00700509 / $15.99
VOL. 96 – BEST COUNTRY HITS	00211615 / $16.99
VOL. 97 – CHRISTMAS CLASSICS	00236542 / $14.99
VOL. 99 – ZZ TOP	00700762 / $16.99
VOL. 100 – B.B. KING	00700466 / $16.99
VOL. 101 – SONGS FOR BEGINNERS	00701917 / $14.99
VOL. 102 – CLASSIC PUNK	00700769 / $14.99
VOL. 104 – DUANE ALLMAN	00700846 / $22.99
VOL. 105 – LATIN	00700939 / $16.99
VOL. 106 – WEEZER	00700958 / $17.99
VOL. 107 – CREAM	00701069 / $17.99
VOL. 108 – THE WHO	00701053 / $17.99
VOL. 109 – STEVE MILLER	00701054 / $19.99
VOL. 110 – SLIDE GUITAR HITS	00701055 / $17.99
VOL. 111 – JOHN MELLENCAMP	00701056 / $14.99
VOL. 112 – QUEEN	00701052 / $16.99
VOL. 113 – JIM CROCE	00701058 / $19.99
VOL. 114 – BON JOVI	00701060 / $17.99
VOL. 115 – JOHNNY CASH	00701070 / $17.99
VOL. 116 – THE VENTURES	00701124 / $17.99
VOL. 117 – BRAD PAISLEY	00701224 / $16.99
VOL. 118 – ERIC JOHNSON	00701353 / $17.99
VOL. 119 – AC/DC CLASSICS	00701356 / $19.99
VOL. 120 – PROGRESSIVE ROCK	00701457 / $14.99
VOL. 121 – U2	00701508 / $17.99
VOL. 122 – CROSBY, STILLS & NASH	00701610 / $16.99
VOL. 123 – LENNON & McCARTNEY ACOUSTIC	00701614 / $16.99
VOL. 124 – SMOOTH JAZZ	00200664 / $16.99
VOL. 125 – JEFF BECK	00701687 / $19.99
VOL. 126 – BOB MARLEY	00701701 / $17.99
VOL. 127 – 1970s ROCK	00701739 / $17.99
VOL. 128 – 1960s ROCK	00701740 / $14.99
VOL. 129 – MEGADETH	00701741 / $17.99
VOL. 130 – IRON MAIDEN	00701742 / $17.99
VOL. 131 – 1990s ROCK	00701743 / $14.99
VOL. 132 – COUNTRY ROCK	00701757 / $15.99
VOL. 133 – TAYLOR SWIFT	00701894 / $16.99
VOL. 135 – MINOR BLUES	00151350 / $17.99
VOL. 136 – GUITAR THEMES	00701922 / $14.99
VOL. 137 – IRISH TUNES	00701966 / $15.99
VOL. 138 – BLUEGRASS CLASSICS	00701967 / $17.99

VOL. 139 – GARY MOORE	00702370 / $17.99
VOL. 140 – MORE STEVIE RAY VAUGHAN	00702396 / $19.99
VOL. 141 – ACOUSTIC HITS	00702401 / $16.99
VOL. 142 – GEORGE HARRISON	00237697 / $17.99
VOL. 143 – SLASH	00702425 / $19.99
VOL. 144 – DJANGO REINHARDT	00702531 / $17.99
VOL. 145 – DEF LEPPARD	00702532 / $19.99
VOL. 146 – ROBERT JOHNSON	00702533 / $16.99
VOL. 147 – SIMON & GARFUNKEL	14041591 / $17.99
VOL. 148 – BOB DYLAN	14041592 / $17.99
VOL. 149 – AC/DC HITS	14041593 / $19.99
VOL. 150 – ZAKK WYLDE	02501717 / $19.99
VOL. 151 – J.S. BACH	02501730 / $16.99
VOL. 152 – JOE BONAMASSA	02501751 / $24.99
VOL. 153 – RED HOT CHILI PEPPERS	00702990 / $19.99
VOL. 155 – ERIC CLAPTON UNPLUGGED	00703085 / $17.99
VOL. 156 – SLAYER	00703770 / $19.99
VOL. 157 – FLEETWOOD MAC	00101382 / $17.99
VOL. 159 – WES MONTGOMERY	00102593 / $22.99
VOL. 160 – T-BONE WALKER	00102641 / $17.99
VOL. 161 – THE EAGLES ACOUSTIC	00102659 / $19.99
VOL. 162 – THE EAGLES HITS	00102667 / $17.99
VOL. 163 – PANTERA	00103036 / $19.99
VOL. 164 – VAN HALEN: 1986-1995	00110270 / $19.99
VOL. 165 – GREEN DAY	00210343 / $17.99
VOL. 166 – MODERN BLUES	00700764 / $16.99
VOL. 167 – DREAM THEATER	00111938 / $24.99
VOL. 168 – KISS	00113421 / $17.99
VOL. 169 – TAYLOR SWIFT	00115982 / $16.99
VOL. 170 – THREE DAYS GRACE	00117337 / $16.99
VOL. 171 – JAMES BROWN	00117420 / $16.99
VOL. 172 – THE DOOBIE BROTHERS	00119670 / $17.99
VOL. 173 – TRANS-SIBERIAN ORCHESTRA	00119907 / $19.99
VOL. 174 – SCORPIONS	00122119 / $19.99
VOL. 175 – MICHAEL SCHENKER	00122127 / $17.99
VOL. 176 – BLUES BREAKERS WITH JOHN MAYALL & ERIC CLAPTON	00122132 / $19.99
VOL. 177 – ALBERT KING	00123271 / $17.99
VOL. 178 – JASON MRAZ	00124165 / $17.99
VOL. 179 – RAMONES	00127073 / $16.99
VOL. 180 – BRUNO MARS	00129706 / $16.99
VOL. 181 – JACK JOHNSON	00129854 / $16.99
VOL. 182 – SOUNDGARDEN	00138161 / $17.99
VOL. 183 – BUDDY GUY	00138240 / $17.99
VOL. 184 – KENNY WAYNE SHEPHERD	00138258 / $17.99
VOL. 185 – JOE SATRIANI	00139457 / $19.99
VOL. 186 – GRATEFUL DEAD	00139459 / $17.99
VOL. 187 – JOHN DENVER	00140839 / $19.99
VOL. 188 – MÖTLEY CRÜE	00141145 / $19.99
VOL. 189 – JOHN MAYER	00144350 / $19.99
VOL. 190 – DEEP PURPLE	00146152 / $19.99
VOL. 191 – PINK FLOYD CLASSICS	00146164 / $17.99
VOL. 192 – JUDAS PRIEST	00151352 / $19.99
VOL. 193 – STEVE VAI	00156028 / $19.99
VOL. 194 – PEARL JAM	00157925 / $17.99
VOL. 195 – METALLICA: 1983-1988	00234291 / $22.99
VOL. 196 – METALLICA: 1991-2016	00234292 / $19.99

Prices, contents, and availability subject to change without notice.

HAL•LEONARD®
www.halleonard.com

0222
173

RE-ORDED VER-IONS®
The Best Note-For-Note Transcriptions Available

AUTHENTIC TRANSCRIPTIONS WITH NOTES AND TABLATURE

00690603	Aerosmith – O Yeah! Ultimate Hits ...	$29.99
00690178	Alice in Chains – Acoustic	$22.99
00694865	Alice in Chains – Dirt	$19.99
00694925	Alice in Chains – Jar of Flies/Sap	$19.99
00691091	Alice Cooper – Best of	$24.99
00690958	Duane Allman – Guitar Anthology	$29.99
00694932	Allman Brothers Band – Volume 1	$29.99
00694933	Allman Brothers Band – Volume 2	$27.99
00694934	Allman Brothers Band – Volume 3	$29.99
00690945	Alter Bridge – Blackbird	$24.99
00123558	Arctic Monkeys – AM	$24.99
00214869	Avenged Sevenfold – Best of 2005-2013	$24.99
00690489	Beatles – 1	$24.99
00694929	Beatles – 1962-1966	$27.99
00694930	Beatles – 1967-1970	$29.99
00694880	Beatles – Abbey Road	$19.99
00694832	Beatles – Acoustic Guitar	$27.99
00690110	Beatles – White Album (Book 1)	$19.99
00692385	Chuck Berry	$24.99
00147787	Black Crowes – Best of	$24.99
00690149	Black Sabbath	$19.99
00690901	Black Sabbath – Best of	$22.99
00691010	Black Sabbath – Heaven and Hell	$22.99
00690148	Black Sabbath – Master of Reality	$19.99
00690142	Black Sabbath – Paranoid	$17.99
00148544	Michael Bloomfield – Guitar Anthology	$24.99
00158600	Joe Bonamassa – Blues of Desperation	$24.99
00198117	Joe Bonamassa – Muddy Wolf at Red Rocks	$24.99
00283540	Joe Bonamassa – Redemption	$24.99
00358863	Joe Bonamassa – Royal Tea	$24.99
00690913	Boston	$19.99
00690491	David Bowie – Best of	$22.99
00286503	Big Bill Broonzy – Guitar Collection	$19.99
00690261	The Carter Family Collection	$19.99
00691079	Johnny Cash – Best of	$24.99
00690936	Eric Clapton – Complete Clapton	$34.99
00694869	Eric Clapton – Unplugged	$24.99
00124873	Eric Clapton – Unplugged (Deluxe)	$29.99
00138731	Eric Clapton & Friends – The Breeze	$24.99
00139967	Coheed & Cambria – In Keeping Secrets of Silent Earth: 3	$24.99
00141704	Jesse Cook – Works, Vol. 1	$19.99
00288787	Creed – Greatest Hits	$22.99
00690819	Creedence Clearwater Revival	$27.99
00690648	Jim Croce – Very Best of	$19.99
00690572	Steve Cropper – Soul Man	$22.99
00690613	Crosby, Stills & Nash – Best of	$29.99
00690784	Def Leppard – Best of	$24.99
00694831	Derek and the Dominos – Layla & Other Assorted Love Songs	$24.99
00291164	Dream Theater – Distance Over Time	$24.99
00278631	Eagles – Greatest Hits 1971-1975	$22.99
00278632	Eagles – Very Best of	$39.99
00690515	Extreme II – Pornograffitti	$24.99
00150257	John Fahey – Guitar Anthology	$24.99
00690664	Fleetwood Mac – Best of	$24.99
00691024	Foo Fighters – Greatest Hits	$24.99
00120220	Robben Ford – Guitar Anthology	$29.99
00295410	Rory Gallagher – Blues	$24.99
00139460	Grateful Dead – Guitar Anthology	$29.99
00691190	Peter Green – Best of	$24.99

00287517	Greta Van Fleet – Anthem of the Peaceful Army	$19.99
00287515	Greta Van Fleet – From the Fires	$19.99
00694798	George Harrison – Anthology	$24.99
00692930	Jimi Hendrix – Are You Experienced?	$29.99
00692931	Jimi Hendrix – Axis: Bold As Love	$24.99
00690304	Jimi Hendrix – Band of Gypsys	$24.99
00694944	Jimi Hendrix – Blues	$29.99
00692932	Jimi Hendrix – Electric Ladyland	$27.99
00660029	Buddy Holly – Best of	$24.99
00200446	Iron Maiden – Guitar Tab	$29.99
00694912	Eric Johnson – Ah Via Musicom	$24.99
00690271	Robert Johnson – Transcriptions	$27.99
00690427	Judas Priest – Best of	$24.99
00690492	B.B. King – Anthology	$29.99
00130447	B.B. King – Live at the Regal	$19.99
00690134	Freddie King – Collection	$22.99
00327968	Marcus King – El Dorado	$22.99
00690157	Kiss – Alive	$19.99
00690356	Kiss – Alive II	$24.99
00291163	Kiss – Very Best of	$24.99
00345767	Greg Koch – Best of	$29.99
00690377	Kris Kristofferson – Guitar Collection	$22.99
00690834	Lamb of God – Ashes of the Wake	$24.99
00690525	George Lynch – Best of	$29.99
00690955	Lynyrd Skynyrd – All-Time Greatest Hits	$24.99
00694954	Lynyrd Skynyrd – New Best of	$24.99
00690577	Yngwie Malmsteen – Anthology	$29.99
00694896	John Mayall with Eric Clapton – Blues Breakers	$19.99
00694952	Megadeth – Countdown to Extinction	$24.99
00276065	Megadeth – Greatest Hits: Back to the Start	$24.99
00694951	Megadeth – Rust in Peace	$27.99
00690011	Megadeth – Youthanasia	$24.99
00209876	Metallica – Hardwired to Self-Destruct	$24.99
00690646	Pat Metheny – One Quiet Night	$24.99
00102591	Wes Montgomery – Guitar Anthology	$27.99
00691092	Gary Moore – Best of	$27.99
00694802	Gary Moore – Still Got the Blues	$24.99
00355456	Alanis Morisette – Jagged Little Pill	$22.99
00690611	Nirvana	$24.99
00694913	Nirvana – In Utero	$22.99
00694883	Nirvana – Nevermind	$19.99
00690026	Nirvana – Unplugged in New York	$19.99
00265439	Nothing More – Tab Collection	$24.99
00243349	Opeth – Best of	$22.99
00690499	Tom Petty – Definitive Guitar Collection	$29.99
00121933	Pink Floyd – Acoustic Guitar Collection	$27.99
00690428	Pink Floyd – Dark Side of the Moon	$22.99
00244637	Pink Floyd – Guitar Anthology	$24.99
00239799	Pink Floyd – The Wall	$24.99
00690789	Poison – Best of	$22.99
00690925	Prince – Very Best of	$24.99
00690003	Queen – Classic Queen	$24.99
00694975	Queen – Greatest Hits	$25.99
00694910	Rage Against the Machine	$22.99
00119834	Rage Against the Machine – Guitar Anthology	$24.99
00690426	Ratt – Best of	$24.99
00690055	Red Hot Chili Peppers – Blood Sugar Sex Magik	$19.99

00690379	Red Hot Chili Peppers – Californication	$22.99
00690673	Red Hot Chili Peppers – Greatest Hits	$22.99
00690852	Red Hot Chili Peppers – Stadium Arcadium	$29.99
00690511	Django Reinhardt – Definitive Collection	$24.99
00690014	Rolling Stones – Exile on Main Street	$24.99
00690631	Rolling Stones – Guitar Anthology	$34.99
00323854	Rush – The Spirit of Radio: Greatest Hits, 1974-1987	$22.99
00173534	Santana – Guitar Anthology	$29.99
00276350	Joe Satriani – What Happens Next	$24.99
00690566	Scorpions – Best of	$24.99
00690604	Bob Seger – Guitar Collection	$24.99
00234543	Ed Sheeran – Divide*	$19.99
00691114	Slash – Guitar Anthology	$34.99
00690813	Slayer – Guitar Collection	$24.99
00690419	Slipknot	$19.99
00316982	Smashing Pumpkins – Greatest Hits	$22.99
00690912	Soundgarden – Guitar Anthology	$24.99
00120004	Steely Dan – Best of	$27.99
00322564	Stone Temple Pilots – Thank You	$22.99
00690520	Styx – Guitar Collection	$22.99
00120081	Sublime	$19.99
00690531	System of a Down – Toxicity	$19.99
00694824	James Taylor – Best of	$19.99
00694887	Thin Lizzy – Best of	$22.99
00253237	Trivium – Guitar Tab Anthology	$24.99
00690683	Robin Trower – Bridge of Sighs	$19.99
00156024	Steve Vai – Guitar Anthology	$34.99
00660137	Steve Vai – Passion & Warfare	$29.99
00295076	Van Halen – 30 Classics	$29.99
00690024	Stevie Ray Vaughan – Couldn't Stand the Weather	$19.99
00660058	Stevie Ray Vaughan – Lightnin' Blues 1983-1987	$29.99
00217455	Stevie Ray Vaughan – Plays Slow Blues	$24.99
00694835	Stevie Ray Vaughan – The Sky Is Crying	$24.99
00690015	Stevie Ray Vaughan – Texas Flood	$22.99
00694789	Muddy Waters – Deep Blues	$27.99
00152161	Doc Watson – Guitar Anthology	$24.99
00690071	Weezer (The Blue Album)	$22.99
00237811	White Stripes – Greatest Hits	$24.99
00117511	Whitesnake – Guitar Collection	$24.99
00122303	Yes – Guitar Collection	$24.99
00690443	Frank Zappa – Hot Rats	$22.99
00121684	ZZ Top – Early Classics	$27.99
00690589	ZZ Top – Guitar Anthology	$24.99

COMPLETE SERIES LIST ONLINE!

HAL•LEONARD®
www.halleonard.com

Prices and availability subject to change without notice.
*Tab transcriptions only.

0122
272